A Child's Day In ...

My Life in
JAMAICA

Patience Coster

W
FRANKLIN WATTS
LONDON • SYDNEY

First published in 2015 by Franklin Watts

Copyright © Arcturus Holdings Limited

Franklin Watts
338 Euston Road
London
NW1 3BH

Franklin Watts Australia
Level 17/207 Kent Street, Sydney, NSW 2000

Produced by Arcturus Publishing Limited,
26/27 Bickels Yard, 151–153 Bermondsey Street, London SE1 3HA

Editor: Joe Harris
Designer: Ian Winton

Picture credits:
All photography courtesy of Andrew P. Smith/Demotix/Corbis

A CIP catalogue record for this book is available from the British Library.

Dewey Decimal Classification Number: 972.9'206

ISBN: 978 1 4451 3740 7

Franklin Watts is a division of Hachette Children's Books, an Hachette UK company.
www.hachette.co.uk

Printed in China

SL004301UK

Supplier 03, Date 1014, Print Run 3570

Contents

My home 4

Breakfast 6

Time to go 8

The school bus 10

My school 12

Lessons begin 14

Break time 16

Maths class 18

Lunchtime 20

Afternoon lessons 22

Dance class 24

Shopping 26

Dinner and bedtime 28

Glossary 30

Further information 31

Index 32

My home

Hi! My name is Zola. I live in Liguanea, a town on the outskirts of Kingston, Jamaica. I am ten years old.

There are four people in my family – Dad, Mum, my little sister Tany and me. I share a bedroom with Tany.

Zola says ...

Our bedroom is crowded. Sometimes it's hard to find stuff!

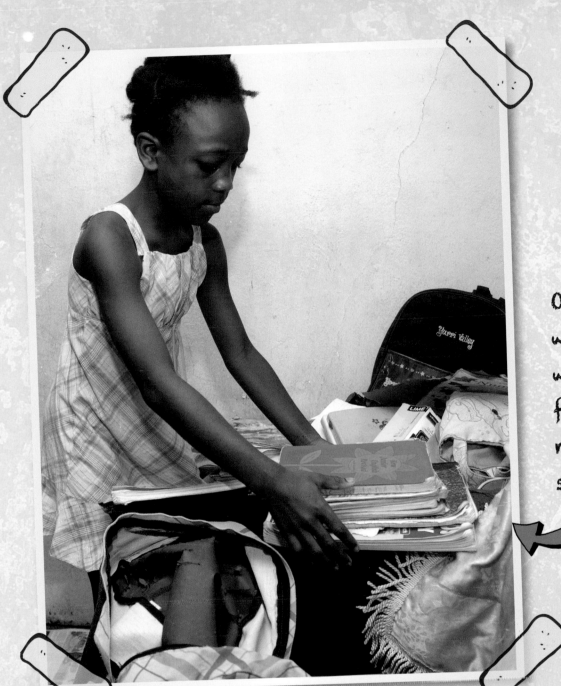

Oh, that's where they were! I've found all my books for school today.

My country

Jamaica is a mountainous island in the Caribbean Sea. Around three million people live here. One third of all Jamaicans live in the capital city, Kingston.

Breakfast

Before breakfast, I wash and get dressed. Like most children in Jamaica, I wear a uniform to school.

My uniform is a brown skirt and tie, with the school emblem, and a white short-sleeved shirt.

Dad fries pancakes for breakfast. On other days we might have boiled bananas, potatoes or yams. While breakfast is cooking, Dad gets my packed lunch together.

Zola says ...

I always give thanks for my food before eating.

Starting the day

In Jamaica most people eat cooked breakfasts. Some people have fried or boiled eggs with cornmeal or banana porridge.

Time to go

Mum works until late at a factory, so Dad is in charge of getting us to school in the mornings.

I play a quick game with Tany on my mobile phone. She will be starting school next term.

Dad gives me money for the bus and to buy a snack.

Mum makes sure my hair is tidy before I leave.

Money and schooling

The Jamaican government wants every child to be in school. However, some families can't afford the bus fare to send their children to school.

The school bus

Dad walks with me to the bus stop. It is just a short walk from my house and the journey to school only takes five minutes.

The school day starts at 8 o'clock. Dad is worried that we won't make it to the bus stop on time!

The bus takes students to the primary and senior schools – it can get quite crowded and hot!

Zola says ...

I told you we would make it on time, Dad!

Climate

Jamaica is close to the equator. It has a tropical climate, which means it is hot and humid all year round. It is sometimes hit by hurricanes in the summer months.

My school

The name of my school is St Francis Primary and Infant School. Around 900 children attend the school. There are **48** students in my class.

I wait with my friend Leon for the teacher to arrive.

Each day we have different responsibilities. We might be in charge of class devotion or collecting the books at the end of a lesson.

Zola says ...

For devotion, we take it in turns to read a passage from the Bible out loud.

Religion in Jamaica

St Francis is a Roman Catholic school. It was founded by Catholic nuns in 1890. Nowadays, 62 per cent of people in Jamaica are Protestants.

Lessons begin

We take our seats for the first lesson of the day, which is science. Today we are learning about air pollution.

Jamaica is a famously beautiful country. Tourists travel here from all over the world. However, like many countries, we have problems with pollution.

Zola says ...

We all have a lot to say about this subject!

The teacher asks us to think about how we can stop pollution. We split into small study groups.

Primary education

In Jamaica we attend primary school for six years, between the ages of six and 11. All our lessons are taught in English.

Break time

10.00 AM

At break time, we all go out to the yard to chat and play. It's a hot day, so we stay in the shade.

Dad has packed me an orange for my snack. It has been grown right here in Jamaica... and it's delicious!

Zola says ...

Mary is my best friend. We are always laughing when we are together.

My friend Lisa hasn't brought a drink, so I share my juice with her. On a day like today, even standing around talking can be thirsty work!

Jamaican farms

Jamaican crops such as sugar, rum, coffee, bananas and yams are shipped all over the world. Jamaica's farms are very important, because they bring money into the country.

17

Maths class

After break, we have maths. I like adding and subtracting, but find some things, like multiplying decimals, quite hard.

I get a bit stuck when I have to work out sums in front of the class.

Our teacher, Mrs Blake-Palmer, gets us to sing a song about maths to make us more confident.

Zola says ...

We sing the song to the tune of Bob Marley's 'Three Little Birds'.

Jamaican music

Jamaican musician Bob Marley was famous for a type of music called reggae. Reggae has been around since 1960. It's a kind of dance music with a bouncy beat. Other types of music that started out in Jamaica include ska and dancehall.

Lunchtime

Around noon I eat my packed lunch in the classroom. Today I have a beef patty. Then I hang out with my friends Mary and Rashona in the yard.

We play handclapping games like 'Four White Horses' and 'Lemonade Crunchy Ice'.

Zola says ...
We sing or chant a song as we clap in rhythm – it's good fun!

20

When lunchtime is over, we line up and say a prayer before going back into class. We have to be really still and quiet!

Playground games

If someone remembers to bring a rope or two, we play double-dutch skipping and sometimes handball. S-T-O-P is another handclap game, which is a version of dodge or tag.

Afternoon lessons

After lunch we are all back in class to practise our reading. Then we have lessons in language arts and music.

In language arts we are learning how to talk and write about friendship.

In music we are listening to examples and learning how to recognize written notes and symbols.

The school day ends at 2:30PM. We are all dismissed and I go to catch the bus home.

Zola says ...
I'm glad it's not far to the bus stop - my school books are heavy!

Languages

Jamaica is an English-speaking country. We also speak Jamaican patois, which mixes together words from English and African languages.

Dance class

On Monday evenings I go to a dance class at a nearby church. When I get home I have some crackers and cheese. Then I change into my dance clothes.

We are practising for a performance at this Sunday's church service.

We do warm-up exercises first.

Zola says ...
I love to dance with other people – it's like a game!

Last month our group won a gold medal at the national schools' dance competition.

Folk dances

There are many traditional Jamaican folk dances. Some, such as the maypole dance, originate in Europe. Others, such as jonkunnu, dinki-mini and maroon, originated in Africa.

Shopping

Dad brings Tany along to collect me from dance class. We go to a supermarket to pick up some groceries.

We need to buy a drink for my packed lunch tomorrow.

At the weekend we usually go to the local market to buy fruit and vegetables.

Before dinner I do my maths homework.

Zola says ...

I'm going to keep practising my decimals until I get them right!

Market

Jamaican markets sell different local crafts ranging from batik fabrics and baskets to wood carvings. Dolphin and fish carvings are made from the Jamaican national tree, *lignum vitae*, or tree of life.

7.00 PM

Dinner and bedtime

I eat dinner with Tany. Dad waits for Mum to come home so that they can eat together.

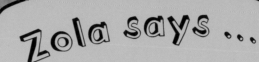

Zola says ...

We have steamed fish with yams and callaloo.

We may watch TV after dinner or play a card game like 'Donkey' or 'Go Fishing'.

Before bed, Tany and I wash our faces, clean our teeth and say our prayers.

Food in Jamaica

Jamaican cooking is spicy and tasty. People from many different countries have settled here in the past **400** years. They have all made their mark on the local food! The national dish is salt-fish and ackee.

Glossary

ackee The national fruit of Jamaica — it looks a bit like a lychee.

afford To have enough money to pay for something.

batik A method of using wax on fabrics to create patterns. The waxed areas of the fabric resist the dye, while the unwaxed areas take the dye.

callaloo A Jamaican dish made with a type of spinach, salt and onions.

cornmeal A food made by crushing maize into a powder.

crackers Thin, crispy baked bread products.

devotion Bible class to start the day in school.

double-dutch skipping A type of skipping where two ropes are used turning in opposite directions.

emblem A badge or symbol.

Franciscan A member of a Christian religious order founded by St Francis of Assisi in 1209.

handball A game in which a ball is hit against a wall with the hand.

humid Hot, clammy and damp.

hurricane A storm with a very strong wind that usually causes lots of damage.

patty A small cake of minced food, usually meat.

pollution Allowing something harmful to living things to escape into the air, water or soil.

Protestant A member of the Christian Church that is separate from the Roman Catholic Church.

responsibilities Things that you have to do.

Roman Catholic A Christian Church of which the Pope is the supreme head.

salt-fish A type of fish, usually cod, that has been preserved in salt.

yam The long, thick root of a tropical plant that is eaten as a starchy vegetable, much like a potato or sweet potato.

Further information

Websites

http://jamaicans.com/childsguide/
Culture, recipes, stories and more.

http://kids.nationalgeographic.com/explore/countries/jamaica.html
Facts, geography, nature, people and culture, government,
economy and history.

www.activityvillage.co.uk/jamaica
Information, games and puzzles.

www.everyculture.com/Ja-Ma/Jamaica.html
The history, food, economy and culture of Jamaica.

www.sciencekids.co.nz/sciencefacts/countries/jamaica.html
Facts and figures about Jamaica.

Further reading

Amazing Athletes: Usain Bolt by Jeff Savage (Lerner Publications,
2012)

Caribbean Today: Jamaica by Colleen Williams (Mason Crest
Publishers, 2009)

Country Explorers: Jamaica by Michael Capek (Lerner Publications,
2010)

Letters From Around the World: Jamaica by Alison Brownlie,
(Cherrytree Books, 2009)

Read On: Bound for Jamaica by Gareth Calway (Collins Educations,
2012)

World Alphabet: Jamaica by Benjamin Zephaniah (Frances Lincoln
Children's Books, 2009)

Index

ackee 29
air pollution 12, 13

bananas 7, 17
Bob Marley 19
break time 16–17
breakfast 6–7

callaloo 28
capital city 5
Caribbean Sea 5
class size 12
climate 11
coffee 17
cornmeal 7
crafts 27
crops 17

dancing 24–25
devotion 13
dinner 28

English 15, 23

family 4
farms 17
folk dances 25
food 6–7, 16, 17, 20, 24, 26, 28–29

games 8, 20–21, 28

hurricanes 11

Jamaica 4, 5, 6, 7, 11, 13, 14, 15, 16, 17, 19, 23, 25, 27, 29
Jamaican government 9

Kingston 4, 5

language arts 22
lessons 14–15, 18–19, 22–23
Liguanea 4
lunch 20

manners 9 markets 26–27
maths 18–19, 27
mobile phone 8
music 19, 23

national dish 29
national tree 27

patois 23
population 5
prayers 7, 29
primary school 11, 12, 15
Protestants 13

reggae 19
religion 7, 13, 21
Roman Catholics 13
rum 17

salt-fish 29
school 5, 6, 8, 9, 10, 11, 12–13, 15, 23, 25
school age 15
school bus 9, 10–11, 23
school day 10
science 14, 15
shopping 26–27
study groups 15
sugar 17
summer 11

television 28
tourists 14

uniform 6

work 8

yams 7, 17, 28

Series contents

My Life in BRAZIL

• Waking up • Getting dressed • Walking to school • Lessons begin
• Break time • Back to work! • Lunchtime • More lessons • School's
out • Helping at home • Downtime • Hobbies • Dinner and bedtime

My Life in FRANCE

• My day begins • Going to school • Registration • Morning classes
• Maths lesson • Lunchtime • Back to school • Afternoon classes
• Homework • Baking a cake • Music practice • Playtime
• Dinner and bedtime

My Life in INDIA

• Morning • Getting ready • Going to school • School assembly
• Lessons • Art and music • Sport • Hometime • Lunch • Out and about
• Shopping • At home • Evening meal

My Life in INDONESIA

• Morning • Breakfast • Walking to school • Morning register • Lesson
time • Physical education • Playtime and lunch • Traditional dancing
• Hometime • Music practice • Family shop • At home • Evening meal

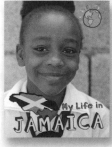

My Life in JAMAICA

• My home • Breakfast • Time to go • The school bus • My school
• Lessons begin • Break time • Maths class • Lunchtime • Afternoon
lessons • Dance class • Shopping • Dinner and bedtime

My Life in KENYA

• Getting up • Breakfast • Walking to school • Lesson time • Playtime
• In the library • Eating lunch • Afternoon lessons • Walking home
• Fetching water • At the market • Evening meal • Going to bed